TENKARA & BAMBOO

The Fisherman and the Tenkara
-
The Art of Fishing with the Ancient Japanese Fly Fishing Technique

Lelio Zeloni

Copyright © 2023 Lelio Zeloni

All rights reserved

ISBN: 978-1-80361-368-0

Author:

Lelio Zeloni was born in Prato on August 8th, 1953. Since he was an adolescent, he has had two passions, painting and fishing. Over the years he has practiced spinning, fly fishing, tenkara and of course his favourite, fishing with bread. These experiences with different techniques, have helped him to become the expert fisherman that he is today.

leliopesca.com

Youtube: Lelio Pesca
Instagram: Lelio Pesca
Facebook: Lelio Pesca

In no event shall any liability or legal responsibility be held against the author, for damages, repairs or monetary losses due to the information contained in this book. Directly or indirectly.

Reproductions made for professional, economic or commercial purposes or for uses other than personal use can only be made following specific authorization issued by the author.

CONTENTS

Preface..5

Introduction..11

1. Techniques Practiced Before Tenkara..................15

2. Artificial Fly Fishing...25

    Fish Behaviors..36

    Wet Fly Fishing..37

    Dry Fly Fishing..39

3. The Half-Flies...43

4. How I Met Tenkara...47

5. The Tenkara...55

    Origins of the Word Tenkara........................57

    The Philosophy and Culture of Tenkara......59

6. Tenkara and Valsesiana....................................65

7. DIY Bamboo Fishing Rod.................................71

    A Moment of Reflection................................72

    Modern Canes and Tips................................78

8. Tenkara Lines...81

9. The Tenkara Flies..83

    Aquatic Insects..86

        Ephemeroptera...88

        Trichoptera..90

        Plecoptera..92

    How to Use the Various Types of Flies.........................95

    Terrestrial Insects..100

        Diptera..100

        Hymenoptera..101

    DIY Flies..102

10. Where to Practice Tenkara?....................................105

11. How to Tackle the Creek the Right Way....................109

12. How to Tenkara Fish..113

    Our Tenkara Rod..114

    How to Prepare the Line................................114

    Casting..115

    Catch & Release...116

Conclusion..119

Bibliographical References..................................123

Preface

What if I started right away by telling you that tenkara is good for the brain? That would be a bit of a bold premise to make in these first few lines, but it would be interesting to find out together whether a passion like fishing can also turn into an activity that is good for your health.

Let's start right away by saying that learning new things is good for you. You may be surprised to learn that lack of novelty weakens the brain. When we went to school we were almost always doing something new. New subjects, new topics, new classmates, new games in the gym and new teachers with new teaching styles. All this helped keep our brains fresh and active.

Unfortunately, many people after school fall into the trap of doing the same things every day. For the brain, this behavior is not virtuous. Routine stifles the creativity of the intellect and impoverishes the vitality of the individual.

By doing the same things over and over again, the brain tends to "shrink," repetitiveness lazes it, so it is very important to always try to do something different to keep it awake.

A brilliant mind is not monotonous and our brain works well if it is stimulated by new things, because using it reinvigorates it, just like a muscle.

So dear fishermen, take advantage of the fishing that gives you the opportunity to do many new things. You can learn new techniques without using the same ones all the time, you can fish in new spots, you can visit new places, and you can embark on catching fish you have never caught before.

This will be revitalizing for your mind and allow you to use your senses in a new way. Being open to change, being curious and learning new things allows us to experience more emotions and experience stimulating situations. All of this helps to strengthen synapses between neurons, regrow dendrites, and stimulate the production of neurotrophins that help the survival, development, and function of neurons. Because the amazing thing is that neurons develop not only in the brains of children, but also in the brains of adults.

So try to always go in search of new things, try to change your fishing, vary your techniques, change your lines, your baits, always go to new places and try to catch different fish.

Be careful of falling into the trap of routine; always challenge yourself with exciting new challenges.

When you break the routine, you change the patterns that have become fixed in your mind and train the brain to deal with new situations. You thus process information in a new way and make the brain more elastic in adapting to changes. You will thus improve your mental elasticity and the neuroplasticity of your brain.

But your enjoyable mental training fortunately does not end there, because you can also engage in DIYs, just as the fishermen of old used to do.

Devoting yourself to DIY fishing is definitely a great mental workout because it is an activity that stimulates the brain, creativity, logic and ingenuity. When you do activities like these that stimulate the intellect, the structure of the brain changes, the gray matter grows and the white matter improves. And this of course has a positive effect on all other aspects of life, because everything we do involves our brain.

We have just learned with pleasure how an activity like fishing can be healthy and help the brain stay young and resilient.

But there is even more, the benefits did not end there, because often going fishing coincides with being in the midst of nature. A pure and unspoiled dimension where natural order reigns. Just what you need to get rid of stress, relax and breathe good air.

You may be surprised to know that the mere sight of water – whether it is a sea, lake, river or stream –

gives relief and calms the mind on a subconscious level. Being near water makes one more relaxed and calm, and it is now proven that people near a waterway and in the open air are more serene and happy.

After reading these first few pages, I bet you felt like going fishing in the wild! That's great! But who knows then what a craving you will have after reading the whole book!

Remember, however, that it will not matter what your next fishing destination is. Nor will it matter how many fish you catch. The most important thing of all is to learn to enjoy the journey.

Smile as you leave the house with your equipment, and try to savor every single moment of your journey. Enjoy the scenery, ignite your senses, smell the scents of the river and the flowers, listen to the song of the stream and the sounds of nature as you are caressed by that light and pleasant gentle breeze. Enjoy every single moment of your fishing day and your life.

Because in the end, it won't matter where we go, but

enjoying every moment of this extraordinary journey called life is the most important thing of all.

Dr. Edoardo Zeloni Magelli

Introduction

I have always fished with different techniques in my life, and I thought I knew a lot about fishing. Many of you will know me from my breadfishing in the sea, but I have always fished in fresh water as well. I used to alternate my outings by spinning, fly fishing, and sometimes free fishing with an earthworm line. These were the techniques that gave me the most excitement.

Then one day when you least expect it, the name of another technique comes tiptoeing in: tenkara. At first I didn't give it much importance. but as time went on, practicing it won me over.

I must admit that practicing fly fishing has made my impact with tenkara much easier. In fly fishing I used to build my own endings with the various decreasing lengths, starting from 0.45 and going up to the 0.14 end, I would also build myself various types of ephemerals and nymphs. Despite the pleasure of self-building I found that all this took a lot of my time, sometimes I lacked the time to devote to all this.

In tenkara this does not occur, because it is all much more practical, simple and less demanding, but most of all it is a lot of fun. Thinking about it is everything that every fisherman subconsciously seeks. And without realizing it I had finally found it.

It is very important for an angler to have a good understanding of different fishing techniques, as this will greatly increase his wealth of experience. In difficult fishing situations he will always be able to understand what is not working at that moment and why.

I would like you to pay close attention to these pages, especially the initial ones, because in them I will decant all my experience.

I will describe the techniques I have practiced, and in

each one there is a piece of advice, a message that will help you improve. It will be as if you experienced them firsthand.

My fishing is very simple and affordable, however, I guarantee that it is very effective. In my humble opinion, for fishing to work it must be kept simple.

But now it is time to begin our journey, and I feel I owe it to you, since we share the same passion, to try to pass on to you all that I have been able to learn.

In a short time you too will become proficient in the tenkara technique, but most importantly you will have a great time and look forward to returning to fishing again.

1.

Techniques Practiced Before Tenkara

As a boy, the first technique I practiced was no-reel fishing, both in the sea and in fresh water. It is the foundation for every angler and all subsequent techniques. Since it is not complicated, it is learned in a short time, and it gives some very fun and pleasant moments to remember.

As you continue to practice it you become a master of the technique, however you feel the need in some spots to have to change something, you feel the need to have to fish farther from shore and make longer passes. So it was that I decided to buy a reel rod. I was very satisfied, I could explore much wider stretches of river and fish deeper in lakes. Also, thanks to a rod with a reel, the sea gives you many different ways to be able to fish and you can exploit it in different spots.

Time passed very pleasantly and as I read various fishing magazines, I became more and more intrigued by the technique of Spinning. I often repeated to myself:

> *"How can a fish bite a spoon! It's just a spinning piece of metal, it's not possible, if that were the case I would have solved the bait problem, I would always have it with me at hand, and I could decide at any time to go fishing."*

Fascinated by this doubt, I decided to try the spinning technique as well. I bought a slender rod with a reel and a few spoons from Mepps, which was called "Mister Fish" in the mail-order catalog.

Once the spinning equipment arrived, I couldn't wait to be able to try it out.

One fine spring Sunday the opportunity immediately presented itself, and together with my wife we decided to go on a picnic to the Suviana reservoir-an artificial lake located in the Bologna Apennines-and of course I brought along the spinning equipment I had purchased.

In the early afternoon I decided even though I was a bit hesitant to try it. I assembled the rod, it was an elegant two-piece plug-in whip, it was very light and measured 150 cm overall. The reel was a Jubilant and was loaded with 0.22 thread.

I tied a carabiner and from the box of spoons took the silver Mepps number 2 silver one and started casting.

As I retrieved the artificial in a very linear fashion and when it was a few meters away from me, I noticed the reflection of the artificial in the water. By this time the first cast had gone awry, so I was thinking of relaunching again, when suddenly I heard a thump on the tip of the rod and saw the silhouette of a lured fish trying to escape causing me to shake the whole rod.

For a moment I was almost incredulous, not

expecting that there, right next to me was a fish willing to bite.

"Then it really works! Unbelievable!"

I exclaimed, as my heart pounded with excitement.

It was the first fish caught by spinning; just think about it! I was over the moon, as I retrieved that fish toward me, I noticed red dots on its body, and with enormous satisfaction I realized that it was a brown trout.

What I had seen in fishing magazines and had always imagined I too could accomplish was materializing right before my eyes; I could touch a brown trout!

After several casts I hooked another one and was already anticipating the second catch when suddenly I felt the rod give way and come toward me. It had dislodged!

I must confess that I was a little disappointed by this loss, but after all, on reflection, it had not gone so badly, because on my first spinning fishing trip I had managed to hook two trout, practicing a new technique that I was completely unfamiliar with. Loaded with confidence, the following weekend, I went to the Pavana reservoir, a small artificial lake in the Tuscan-Emilian Apennines.

Fishing with the same gear this time, I did not catch trout, but rather perch. My experience was increasing from time to time, and every new fishing spot I tried gave me wonderful thrills.

Summer came, and I was on vacation with my family in Donoratico on the Livorno coast in Tuscany. We liked to spend time in nature in tranquility breathing good air away from the city. We had found a beautiful campsite, it was a natural forest behind some maritime dunes overlooking the sea.

I had made some new friends, and in talking with them, I learned about a small pond within the countryside. This pond was used by the farmers for irrigation and they had no objection to someone going fishing in it from time to time.

One afternoon I went fishing in that pond. I was

moved by a strong curiosity because I did not know what fish I would find there, and guided by my instincts, I decided to try spinning fishing.

From the box of spoons I chose a 2 gram copper-plated rotary and began casting. My instincts advised me well, because after a few casts I managed to catch a Black Bass. More casts followed and I caught yet another Bass.

Day by day, more and more different species of the fish I was catching increased, all of which made me feel more experienced, because I was learning to notice the different types of fish biting. Each fish had a different way of biting.

There was one fish that I had never been able to catch, either with natural bait or by spinning. This fish was the chub. For various reasons it had become an obsession.

I read in fishing magazines that he was very cunning, the line had to be very light, the nylon very thin, the lead almost invisible, and that we had to tiptoe up the river because he would hear us. All this only increased in me the figure of an impossible fish to catch. Every time I went fishing and didn't catch a chub, I felt like a beginner.

I was reading articles in magazines about spinning chubs and noticed a very interesting blurb that caught my attention and intrigued me. This blurb said that chubs in the summertime go crazy for the Martin's spinner.

I was immediately reminded of the Bisenzio, the river that runs through my city, Prato. I had never spinning fished in this river and was entertaining the idea of trying it.

Talking about fishing with my brother-in-law Gabriele, it turned out that he used to fish very often by spinning right in the Bisenzio River and also caught beautiful chubs. He knew many good places and invited me to go with him.

You will not believe it, but my brother-in-law at that moment seemed to me to be the savior of the country, the one who can teach you everything and whom I had to watch very well and memorize his every move because I would learn what I still could not understand.

It was thanks to him that I was able to learn how to catch chubs. Thank you Gabriele! Thank you from the bottom of my heart! Many years have passed, but I still carry with me the indelible memory of those extraordinary fishing trips.

In the winter time I fished with the small minnow, while in the summer time I used very small yellow and black Martin spoons. By now I was fishing often in the Byzantium, and I had gotten to know the river.

I particularly remember one January afternoon. The river water was rippling because of a strong north wind, and I was entering the water very slowly with my waders. The good thing about this was that the water moved by the wind hid me from the sight of fish.

It was a magical afternoon, I remember that in the first 5 casts I caught 5 chubs. It was a sign that it was a great time and that I was going to make some good catches. During the fishing I was constantly moving around crossing several very slow streams. In the end I caught a total of 22 chubs and all of them of fair size. This is still to this day my personal record of chubs caught spinning in the Bisenzio. But records are made to be broken aren't they? I am sure I can break it and it would be great to make a video of the fishing trip to share with you through my social channels.

Months passed and I continued to fish. Once again thanks to my brother-in-law Gabriele, I caught a beautiful pike in Lake Bilancino in Mugello. As bait I used a 28-gram Martin spoon with a red bow, and of course I had a nice steel wire.

I was very satisfied with my catches, I had caught as many different species of fish with as many different baits. I was increasingly mastering the technique, by now I had learned it very well and felt the need to want to learn something new again.

2.
Artificial Fly Fishing

Fly fishing is of English origin, there is all the charm of old England in this technique, and slowly, on tiptoe it has managed to conquer the whole world.

The French were the first to get the fly message, managing to fit into the beautiful fishing environment with excellent, state-of-the-art techniques. All of Europe has since followed suit, including Italy.

We must recognize that initially it was a fishing technique reserved for a few people, due to the fact that the equipment was very expensive. Foreign terminology did not make it easy to learn about these artificial flies; the fishing actions themselves were as difficult to understand as the terminology.

Many fishermen considered fly fishing an elite fishery, and those who practiced it often snubbed other techniques.

These were all factors that contributed to keeping the general public away from fly fishing, but fortunately things have changed now.

Knowledge of this technique totally changed my view on fishing, and made me realize that it is not so much the fish we catch that is important, but it is the way we catch them.

I used to often watch movies and documentaries on television. The rods of these fishermen were made of refendu bamboo and had cork handles; they were very beautiful to look at and I was fascinated by the way these fishermen cast the artificial fly. They would spread the rat tail well in the air behind them, and when it was fully extended they would throw it forward again causing the artificial fly to rest gently on the water. They were very peculiar and striking images that in the following days often came to my mind.

"This technique is very beautiful, elegant, has its own charm, I am convinced that it must not be easy to learn it".

I thought.

Hard things have always appealed to me, and so I wanted to challenge myself again. First I bought myself a fly fishing rod, it was made of a carbon blend and measured 8 feet equivalent to about 240 centimeters (a foot is 30.48 cm.). I also bought a DTF5 rat tail and a Daiwa reel and some flies, such as the Red Spinner, March Brown and Coch y Bondhu.

Loaded with enthusiasm, I wanted to attempt the first fishing trip, aware that it would not be easy.

Several times I repeated to myself:

"I have learned the other techniques well, I know fishing, I will learn this technique as well, I just have to give myself the right amount of time it will take to learn."

Arriving on the river, I rigged the rod, threaded the rat tail through the serpentine rings and pulled 3 or 4 more meters of tail from the reel. To this I attached 2 meters of the 0.30 nylon, and on the nylon end I again tied a thinner nylon of about 60 centimeters of 0.14.

I had to choose a fly, and as I watched the insect flies I noticed some tending toward red, so it seemed logical to trigger a Red Spinner as a fly.

Now comes the good stuff.

"How should I cast this fly? Let's focus on casting it!"

I thought.

And so I began to mentally go over in my mind the images I had seen in that beautiful documentary on television at the time.

To raise the tail I did a hint of a double pull, that is, raising the rod with my right hand and at the same time pulling the rat tail toward me with my left hand, trying to spread it well behind me, but no matter how hard I tried, the rat tail always fell into the water wrapping around the entire fly end including the fly.

"There is something wrong!"

I exclaimed.

After many unsuccessful attempts, I reluctantly decided to quit and returned home very disappointed. In the days following that sad experience, I was noticing that the initial fascination I had felt for this technique was slowly fading.

It's not my habit to give up on things even if they don't go right, I had to come up with something to fix it, so I decided to buy a book on fly fishing where it taught this technique the right way.

Thanks to that valuable reading, I understood that I had gotten almost everything wrong. I was getting the construction of the decreasing nylon finials wrong, I was not raising the rod well while casting, and I was not laying the rat tail well behind me so that I could then relaunch it forward.

We can't improvise as casters if we haven't had some

practice first. Casting in fly fishing is very important, it takes a lot of experience, woe betide if we want to do things in a hurry, in the worst case scenario it would mean quitting after a short time and going back to fishing with the usual techniques and baits, such as chiggers and earthworms.

I had to start from scratch and forget everything to get off on the right foot. Fortunately, shortly afterwards it reached my ear that they were holding fly-fishing courses in Prato, at the Giunti Sport Fishing Society. Without delay and without a moment's hesitation I immediately went to enroll.

The course was divided into two parts. The first included theory lessons on everything related to fly fishing, and these lessons were held at the headquarters in the evening after dinner. Then there was the practical part that was held on Saturday afternoon, where casting lessons were given directly on the river. I must admit that these instructors were really good, very patiently passed on to us all their experience in the best way, and thanks to them I really learned what fly fishing is all about.

Once I finished the course, I decided to put what I had learned into practice. Near my house there was a small quarry, where they used to mine clay in its time, and it had become a small pond. When I would observe it in the late afternoon after work, I would often see small circles on the surface of the water-it was the fish bubbling on the insects.

It was the right place to practice what I had learned in the course. It didn't matter to cast far because I could see movement of fish constantly passing between one kelp bank and another.

On the surrounding vegetation I could see dragonflies flying and also many bees; I did not have any flies that resembled these, but it seemed appropriate to try March Brown.

I cast where the kelp beds ended and once in the water made the fly vibrate as if it were alive. These vibrations did not take long to take effect because shortly afterwards I saw a fish leap out of the water with the fly in its mouth and fall noisily back in. It was a Black Bass, not that big, but it was very pugnacious.

What joy, what excitement! I had caught my first fish with an artificial fly, it was the right reward after all the time I had spent learning this wonderful and fascinating technique.

These moments stick in the mind and are never forgotten. I still remember it today as if it were yesterday.

More catches followed, always small fish, but very fun. In addition to Bass that day I also caught rudd and even sun perch.

All right, they are not great catches, but the joy was immense because that day I finally fished the right way and caught different kinds of fish. I understood perfectly that it is not so much the fish you catch, but how you catch them.

When I thought back to the fly-fishing course I had taken, naturally images of the banks of the Bisenzio River came to mind, and my desire to return to those banks to fish grew day by day. And so I did.

I went fishing and arrived on the river and calmly observed the underwater. I immediately noticed chubs moving in and out of the branches of a waterlogged log.

The water was not deep, and a thick bush hid me from their view. These chubs were swimming quietly right below me. I was thinking about the best way to get the fly into the water, which was very transparent.

This situation allowed me to get a good look with my own eyes at how the chub would react to my fly.

From the reel I extracted only about 2 meters of tail, coupling a 0.14-meter leader of about 1 meter. Having seen some insects flying near the vegetation on the light brown, I decided to mount the March Brown as a fly.

I raised my casting arm, and holding the rod high, I made the bush jump to the artificial fly by laying it lightly on the surface of the water. A chub stopped for a moment, turned its head toward the fly and began to observe it.

"I have to shake it slightly to let the fish know that it could have risen up in the air and escaped them!"

I thought.

The chub was slowly approaching the fly and paused for a moment. It was still observing it. Then I made the fly make very small hints of jumps and finally saw the chub open its mouth, suck in the fly and close it again.

"Time to set a hook!"

I thought, and so I did.

Already anticipating the catch, I was about to catch my first chub with an artificial fly and it had all seemed quite easy too. But alas, it didn't turn out that way, I cast, and to my enormous disappointment, I felt the fly come up lightly and saw the chub move away.

"Why!? Why!?"

I have wondered several times.

I have thought so much about this missed catch, I can assure you that it has taught me much more than it should have. Our failures are often our greatest teachers. We can learn a lot from our failures.

Chub is the least desired fish by fly fishermen, yet it is the most fished because it has no closed seasons and is found everywhere. It is a very cunning fish, suspicious, always wary of even the most perfect fly imitation.

Where the water is deep and slow, the chub seizes our artificial from the bottom up, without even breaking the surface of the water, we only notice an imperceptible circle and in a moment it has already released our fly.

One should to pull in advance to catch the right moment, but this is impossible. This is the challenge to the wily cyprinid: to learn well the right moment for shoeing! It takes lots of practice, lots and lots of practice, only then can we take great satisfaction. Consistency always pays off.

Fish Behaviors

After explaining to you the behavior of chub, I want to mention in general how fish behave in the water when they want to get food. These are very important things to know, because based on this we will be able to choose the most suitable fishing method.

All insectivorous fish are affected by the biological cycle of insects.

When we notice the fish in activity on the bottom, it means that it is hunting the larvae and nymphs that have come out into the open from their shelters. In this case, the right imitation to present to the fish will be a small nymph heavily plumbed to get it to the bottom. If we notice that the fish from the bottom rises to the surface, we can infer that a metamorphosis is taking place, and in this case we need to use a less plumbed nymph.

If, on the other hand, the fish rises to the surface and reaches below the water surface, it means that another metamorphosis is taking place. We can use in this case an unplumbed nymph or a submerged fly that will travel below the surface of the water.

When we see circles on the surface, it means that the fish are hunting at the surface of the water – in jargon, the fish are "boiling" - this indicates to us the presence of insects that are completing their development or have already completed their metamorphosis. This is the magic time of dry fly fishing afloat.

These fish behaviors, influenced by insect metamorphosis, tell us which fishing technique to practice. Now you will know how to choose the right technique among these three different techniques: nymph fly fishing, submerged fly fishing and dry fly fishing.

Now let's look in more detail at these last two techniques.

Wet Fly Fishing

This technique is very profitable, we can practice it at any time of the year and in all possible environmental conditions. This might seem at odds with what I said earlier because there is no reference between fish activities and insect metamorphosis.

But let me explain further. Careful observation lets us infer that the fish does not attack our artificial only to get food, but does so for other reasons as well. Well yes, the fish does not attack only for a food issue.

I will preface this by saying that we cannot know a fish's thoughts and know its psychology, but when situations are repeated several times we can determine that there are rules of behavior.

Many times the fish wants to play and is stimulated to play by our artificial. So it can pass by it, push it here and there, and it can get hooked just as it is playing.

Other times it attacks the artificial to defend itself, because this tiny creature has stimulated its territorial defense instincts, or because it has been fooled by the game.

Curiosity also drives the fish to touch this curious

little object with its mouth. Animals are easily intrigued. These are a series of behaviors that have nothing to do with getting food.

I will conclude by telling you that wet fly fishing is done by descending the stream from upstream to downstream.

This will give us better control of the artificial, and we can thus respond more promptly to the bite, even if we sometimes feel that the fish remains lured by itself.

Dry Fly Fishing

While we can practice the wet fly technique practically all year round, dry fly fishing is best practiced in the summertime because we find more concentration of insects in the vicinity of each waterway.

We learn to observe insects, to recognize to the order to which they belong, and above all to pay attention to their shapes and colors, because the closer our imitation comes to the real insect, the easier it will be to convince the fish to bite.

It is the classic boils we see on the water that suggest to us that we are dry fly fishing, all those circles made by the fish that are boiling on the surface alert us that that is the magic moment of dry fly fishing. The fish is in a feeding frenzy, it will confidently pounce on our imitations without a second thought.

The careful fisherman will not miss this golden opportunity and will leave other techniques aside.

Unfortunately, many fishermen snub this activity of observing nature; it is very important before you start fishing to get close to the river and scrutinize the lives of its inhabitants. Those who read well about what is happening at the fishing spot will be rewarded with good catches.

This technique is practiced by going upstream; we have to cast from downstream to upstream, and we can make cross casts or even against the current.

It will be very important to be good at casting our fly

accurately a short distance from where the fish is hunting. By doing so, the current will unsuspectedly and naturally bring our bait in front of the fish's mouth.

Remember that our fly must behave on water like a real insect.

3.
The Half-Flies

One of the most common drawbacks to fishing with natural insects or earthworms is the inability to maintain the shape of the bait over time as the casts succeed one another.

This is because after just a few casts, the bait piles up on the neck or tip of the hook presenting a shapeless set uncovering the nylon knot and the hook headstock.

These are all situations that prevent the fish from biting making our fishing unproductive.

To avoid this serious inconvenience, fortunately, there are half-flies.

What are they? I'll tell you right now!

It is an artificial that half of the hook is covered with silk thread (or cotton thread) to make the body and head with associated hackles (hackles are feathers that are used to make fly fishing ties), while the other half of the hook is primed with live bait, such as chickadees, caterpillars or earthworms.

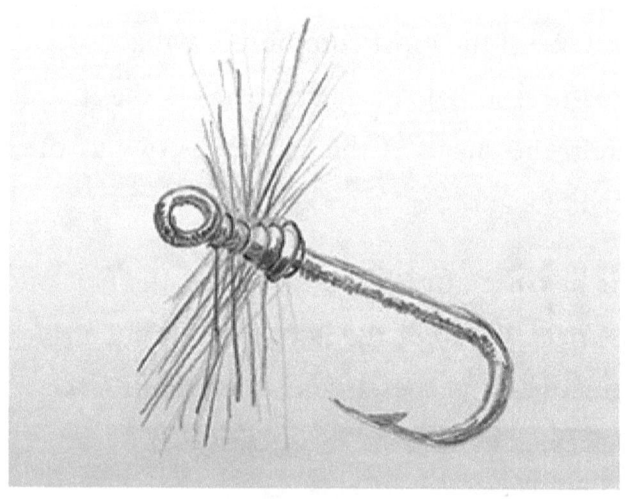

Fig. 1: *The half-fly without live bait.*

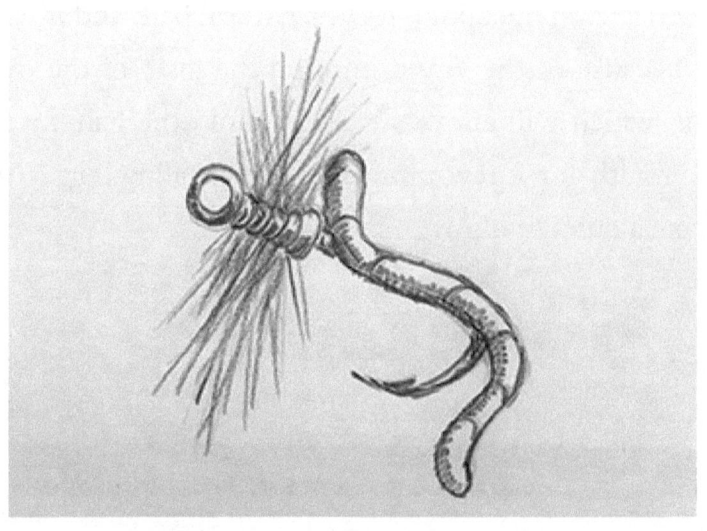

Fig. 2: *The half-fly with live bait.*

The half-fly can also serve another purpose. Many angler friends would like to start fly fishing, are tempted, but they lack the courage to start and do not yet feel ready to abandon live bait for artificial bait.

Well, this very simple technique will ferry you from fishing practiced with live bait to fishing with artificial bait.

You will notice that the fish will quietly take the artificial bait mistaking it for a natural bait, and it will be because of the vibrations and the taste of the live bait, which will allow the fish to hold the half-fly in its mouth for a few moments longer, allowing us to make a quiet hooking.

4.
How I Met Tenkara

I am very grateful toward the half-flies because it was because of them that I was able to hear the word Tenkara for the first time.

I had built myself a yellow silk half-fly with white rooster hackles, to be baited with a maggot.

The Bisenzio was close to home, it was easily accessible, and there were many fish. By now I knew it well; it had become my favorite river. It was the ideal river to experiment with the half-fly technique.

I went to the river, to the edge of a waterfall, where the water flowed fast in the middle, while on the sides it flowed more slowly. At these slower corners there were many stones on the bottom with some rocks outcropping. So it was logical to deduce that there were many refuges for fish.

I set up my 4-meter 50-centimeter no-reel rod with free line, no sinkers or float, tied a half-fly built on a 14-gauge hook, baited with a maggot. I cast into the waterfall, where the water falling from above formed a beautiful white foam, and let the bait drift with the current, holding it under slight tension with the line.

Arriving at the end of the pass I retrieved the half-fly and cast again. As I was carefully checking the line that was passing between two reefs, I suddenly felt a sharp blow and saw the tip of my rod begin to bend more and more.

"I caught it! Half-flies work!"

I said to myself.

After a brief resistance, I brought a chub to shore. Although it was not very big, it had served to give me confidence. In fact, as I continued fishing, I caught yet more chub.

Of course, fishing with free line, without any kind of lead, the cast was very short. I then decided to add a small sinker 30 centimeters from the half-fly so that I could cast farther and let the bait sink a little more.

So, I relaunched the lure again, but this time much farther away. The half-fly caught the current and slowly sank further and further.

The nylon was passing between two outcropping reefs, when suddenly I felt a very sharp blow on the tip of the rod. I quickly realized that it was a bite unlike any other.

"This is not a chub!"

I exclaimed.

I was looking smugly at all the flexibility of the rod, which was very bent at that moment. The fish was holding steadily on the bottom and trying to move upstream.

"I wonder what kind of fish it is..."

I thought.

After a few minutes, I realized that I was right, it was not a chub. When I saw this fish I was a little amazed at first. I immediately noticed its small scales, its greenish brown color it had on its back. It tended to yellow in the sides and almost white in the belly and had a very fleshy mouth from which four wattles hung.

"He's a barbel, that's why he was pulling far and wide!"

I exclaimed.

You won't believe it, but on that half-fly fishing trip – by raying them on the bottom as they were carried by the current – I managed to catch as many as 11 barbel. Plus all those chubs I had fished on the surface without a sinker.

Just imagine. I was delighted because I had practiced a

new technique that I did not know, plus I had caught several fish.

What about tenkara? You may be wondering. Well, during my fishing trip I saw two fishermen advancing in the distance. They were a few dozen meters apart, both fishing with the same technique: one cast, one pause, and go.

They were getting closer and closer to me. I was watching them and mistakenly thought they were fly fishing. When the first angler stood next to me we exchanged a greeting, the classic "Hello, how are you?"

However, in his equipment I noticed something different, he had no reel or rat tail, however, the rod was very nice, it had a cork handle, the color was iridescent black, and it was thin and flexible.

Curious as I am, I asked him questions regarding his rod and how he employed it. He was very kind and told me that he was fishing tenkara, which was much easier than fly fishing because we can move more easily on the river, it is less challenging, and it doesn't matter to be a good casters.

I thanked him for his answers and we said goodbye. Over the next few days I thought back to that fisherman's words and his technique: tenkara.

In an instant I was reminded of distant but very beautiful memories when my son was very young and together we used to watch cartoons on TV. There was one cartoon I followed particularly, it was Sampei, the boy fisherman. I was fascinated by that slender bamboo rod, but even more so by his enthusiasm and the ease with which he could catch fish.

Those videos expressed the joy of fishing, the simplicity of the equipment, and I understood that very little was needed to have fun.

Associating Sampei with what that fisherman had told me, I drew the conclusion that Sampei also fished tenkara. Suddenly I felt a desire to know more. Unfortunately, I could not find anyone who could give me the necessary information. I had to do a lot of research, but I finally managed to find some fairly comprehensive information.

Having been fly fishing for a long time, I had to acknowledge that the impact with tenkara was very easy. But the thing that has excited me the most is the fun, the pure essence of fishing, the newfound joy that this technique can give you.

I cannot know whether the person reading this book is a person who knows little or nothing about tenkara, or is an experienced fisherman. In any case, what I will do in these pages is to try to convey to you everything I know.

5.
The Tenkara

Tenkara is an ancient Japanese fly fishing technique. Its purpose was to catch the various types of trout and char in the various mountain streams. It was not practiced for sport or pastime as we do in our time, but was practiced as a matter of survival. If you caught the fish, you ate, otherwise you skipped the meal.

Fishermen handed down from father to son the secrets that experience had taught them.

The land was rich in bamboo, and it was very easy for them to obtain this material with which they each made their own fishing rod. The fishing line was made from horsehair woven with decreasing twigs. The flies were also made in a very simple and practical way, using readily available materials such as chicken feathers for the hackles and vegetable threads for the body of the fly. But despite this they were very catching flies.

This confirms my theory derived from experience: it is not the fly that matters but it is how you present it to the fish and how you manage to make it come alive.

Tenkara began to become a pastime starting in the 1960s. Before that, it was a matter of survival and profession.

Beginning in the 1980s, it began to spread more and more as a sport thanks in part to the writings of Yamamoto Soseki, who for many is the modern father of tenkara.

Origins of the Word Tenkara

The word tenkara refers to traditional Japanese fly fishing. The origins of the word "tenkara" are shrouded in mystery, partly because there is no actual "kanji" for this word. Kanji are the characters of Chinese origin used in Japanese writing in conjunction with the hiragana and katakana syllabaries.

In any case, there is much evidence that the word tenkara was used to refer to this fly-fishing technique.

In the past, the Kijishi – the artisanal woodcutters in the Tōhoku region of Japan – used the words tegara, tenkara, tengura, tenkarako or tenkako to describe flying insects (Discover Tenkara, n.d.). When referring to fly fishing they used the term *tenkara-tsuri*.

When some Japanese fishing magazines talked about the reel-less fly fishing that Yamamoto Soseki promoted in his books, it was sometimes called *kebari-tsuri*, and sometimes *tenkara* or *tenkara-tsuri*.

Artificial flies for fly fishing used to be called kebari. This word comes from the fusion of two others, the first is *ke* and means feather, while the other is *hari* which means needle, but it can also be translated to fishing hook. In the past, hooks were made from sewing needles, manually bent until the desired shape was obtained, which is why we can accept this double translation. The word *ke* plus *hari* for a pronunciation reason takes the sound of kebari.

Some readers with all these terms could get confused between modern reel fly fishing and classic reel-less fly fishing. Here Yuzo Sebata, another great tenkara master who consolidated the use of the term "tenkara" in Tsuribito (Angler) magazine in the 1980s (Gaskell, 2020), came to the rescue. He explained that the reel-less technique derived from the Shokuryoshi tradition should be called tenkara.

The Shokuryoshi did not fish for fun, they were the fishermen who traded trout, and they did not care about reels because reels were not necessary (Lyle, 2019).

There was no need to cast far in mountain streams

and no need for a reel in the catch. They did as I often do in my fishing videos: they would pull up the rod and take the line in their hands to pull the fish to their feet. The first definition of the word "tenkara" was translated by us Westerners very simply with this meaning: from the sky. The meaning is this: from the sky the flies fall into the water, on which the fish feed, and so it is an acceptable translation that fits perfectly with the natural cycle of the insect and fish feeding. Another similar key is that the fisherman gets his fly into the water from the sky.

The Philosophy and Culture of Tenkara

To refer to tenkara only as a simple and trivial fly-fishing technique would be very reductive and wrong.

The tenkara philosophy preserves and honors many of the values and skills that the mountain professionals had. These included not only the Shokuryoshi, but also the Kijishi who were the woodcutters and wood craftsmen we mentioned earlier.

They produced small turned wooden objects intended for lacquering, as well as ordinary unlacquered bowls, ladles, and trays. They were originally migratory, moving their base of operations from one mountain valley to another every ten years or so. They formed semi-permanent communities where resources allowed by integrating their woodworking with agriculture (Wigen, 1995).

It is easy for us to think that the Kijishi's knowledge and art of woodworking contributed in some way to the construction of excellent fishing rods and the making of those fantastic wooden wading nets of yesteryear.

Among these practitioners were the Matagi, who were the hunters of the mountain forests, also in the Tōhoku region located in northern Japan. They mainly hunted bears.

They prayed before entering the sacred mountain realm, where they spent hours listening, waiting and watching, detecting almost imperceptible signs that a bear is near (National Geographic, 2017). The Matagi still exist today, and they continue to hunt with the same weapons their ancestral ancestors used.

Their culture is centered on their belief in the mountain gods. For them, hunting is a way of life and not a form of sport. Although it may seem like a paradox, their hunting is very respectful and conveys an identity deeply connected to the land and the animals they hunt. After catching their prey, they leave part of the bear's intestines as an offering to the mountain goddess (National Geographic, 2017). Hunted animals are perceived as gifts from the mountain gods.

In some ways we can say that tenkara is the child of these cultures of these mountain professionals.

For example, the Shokuryoshi skillset probably came from the Matagi originally. In fact, the bear-hunting Matagi would often catch iwana (white-spotted char) and move them into headwater streams where there was none or little (Discover Tenkara, n.d.). It was their backup meal if the hunt went wrong for them. These are lessons in fishing and survival that were passed down to these clans of mountain professionals.

One person who embodies this genuine spirit of tenkara is definitely Yuzo Sebata who has dedicated his life to developing and promoting the philosophy and practice of tenkara. He basically invented high-risk and insanely adventurous "genryu" exploration combined with tenkara fishing inspired by the Matagi and Shokuryoshi.

Sebata-san had a great knowledge of the environment, he climbed, swam, foraged and camped for weeks inside the old Matagi caves and shelters like a fearless explorer to access the remotest and most pristine areas of the mountain streams. These sources and springs are called "genryu".

This was Sebata-san's tenkara, the adventurous genryu-tenkara that has inspired many outdoor enthusiasts.

His friends said Sebata-san actually shares the same personality as the iwana he chases (Gaskell, 2020). The iwana is the Japanese name for the white-spotted char, an East Asian trout. These fish have the characteristic of continuing to swim further and further upstream, then upstream, and do so far beyond the limits of Japanese trout and salmon.

Like the white-spotted char, Sebata-san had that unstoppable urge to keep moving further and further upstream to find its limits, as well as to reach – and eventually climb – the obstacle that defeated the iwana in each river system (Tenkara Angler, 2020).

For genryu-tenkara enthusiasts of course fishing is only a small part of the whole experience. It's not just a combination of hiking, climbing and camping, it's something even more extreme like swimming with a backpack where you have everything inside, crossing water with ropes and even survival in difficult terrain.

"Tenkara fishing is very simple, which makes me feel I am a part of the mountains"

Yuzo Sabata

Genryu-tenkara is only one of the variants of tenkara. Beginning in the 1980s, in addition to the spread of traditional tenkara, other daughter techniques of tenkara began to develop. These differed in the rods used at the construction of the line. For example, some accepted the use of level lines.

But although there are different schools, all are based on the skills of the Shokuryoshi who procured food for their families and traded fish.

You may be surprised to know that even today there are tenkara masters who have lived the life of a professional Shokuryoshi. They did not all die out, and some still do today for at least part of their lives (Discover Tenkara, n. d.).

6.

Tenkara and Valsesiana

Tenkara is very similar to our valsesiana, a fly-fishing technique practiced for centuries in Valsesia, an alpine valley in the province of Vercelli in Piedmont at the foot of Monte Rosa.

It, too, is practiced without a reel and involves only a fixed rod, horsehair line and simple flies. It differs from tenkara in only a few details. As in tenkara, the secrets of this fishery have been handed down from father to son.

English fly fishermen fished mainly in calm waters and could cast the bait very far and float it. While in

Valsesia, where there are often fast swirling currents, this was not possible, then a short-distance fishing technique was developed based mainly on the use of wet flies (Pesca Network, 2011).

The valsesiana is a movement fishery and is practiced by ascending, that is, moving upstream up the stream from the valley.

In tenkara, only one one fly is used, while in the Valsesian, 3 flies are usually used, sometimes as many as 4 up to a maximum of 5. These flies tied together form the so-called "Valsesian train," and its length can vary from about 70 to 100 centimeters.

The use of multiple flies is not to try to catch more than one fish at a time, although it may happen occasionally, but it allows us to present flies at different distances and even at different depths in one cast; this helps us cover the water more efficiently.

For example, taking the 3 flies in reference, the top fly fishes on the bottom, the one in the middle fishes in midwater, and the third fishes on the surface. When fishing on the surface, the third fly can also act as a bite marker for the other two. The top fly is held so that it almost dances on the surface of the water, almost like the old American or British technique called "dibbling the top dropper" (Stewart, n.d.).

One normally fishes with three flies spaced about 35 centimeters apart, and the distance depends a lot on the width of the stream and the speed of the water (Boccardo, n.d.).

Flies are usually mounted on grub hooks, which are those that are more arched and curved than the more common ones. In the past, eyeless hooks without eyes were used on which the line was tied and the fly was built directly on it (Boccardo, n.d.).

To make these flies, feathers are usually used that come from the typical game of the Piedmont valleys, such as grey partridge, rock partridge, red-legged partridge, eurasian woodcock, pheasant and thrushes (Boccardo, n.d.).

The flies are strikingly similar to the kebari flies used in tenkara.

As we mentioned earlier, as in tenkara, the line was

constructed from horsehair. It was twisted and braided together in descending order. Then it was made so that it became thinner and thinner toward the end. Usually these braids started from 18-20 horsehair near the tip, down to 2-4. To this end then the Valsesian train was tied.

With flies in Valsesia we can catch different kinds of fish, such as marble trout, brown trout, rainbow trout, Arctic char, brook trout and grayling. Sometimes we can also catch nice chub.

We now conclude by talking about the rod. The Valsesian rod is usually between 3.5 and 4 meters. It can be even longer, such as 4.70 meters, if it is used in valley bottom rivers.

The traditional rod consists of three pieces, the first two made of giant cane (Arundo donax) – a material readily available on riverbanks – while the tip is made of bamboo, because it is more flexible, thin and durable. As an alternative to bamboo, hazel or dogwood (Cornus sanguinea) can be used.

The second piece is the shortest piece and serves as a

connector between the body of the rod and the tip. The latter usually has a length of 50 to 100 centimeters, obviously varying according to the size of the other pieces, and serves to impart strength and sensitivity to the entire rod.

Traditionally, the ligatures in the grafts were made of hemp rope and then passed in pitch, and the whole when finished behaves as one piece, flexible but strong, capable of enabling the catching of fish even weighing a few pounds (Scalvini, n.d.).

Although with many modern variations, it is good to know that these wonderful canes are still being handcrafted in Valsesia. It is very important to maintain and pass on beautiful traditions.

7.
DIY Bamboo Fishing Rod

In this chapter I will give you some very useful tips for those who want to try their hand at making their own bamboo rods. First of all, bamboo should be cut in the winter period, because at that time the sap is stopped.

The cane we need to cut must be at least 4 meters long. A shorter length is no good; it means the cane is not mature enough to be cut. It is advisable to cut several of them, so in case of wastage, we will have more pieces available. Possibly when we are in front of the reedbed, we try to choose the straightest reeds, so we will lose less time when we have to straighten them.

The harvested reeds should be dried and seasoned in a dry, ventilated place. When they are completely dried then we can move on to the straightening stage. We can use any heat source to heat the reed, a fireplace, a gas stove or a brazier, depending on what you have available.

A Moment of Reflection

In this day and age of consumerism, it is rare to see fishermen with wooden rods. This is indeed a pity, because in their simplicity they encapsulate, all the charm of fishing.

Wooden rods blend in well with the environment, they are made of natural material with very little cost, and if a piece breaks, the fisherman himself can replace it very easily. Another nice thing about when people used to make their own rods is that each rod was different because each person customized it according to his or her own taste and skill in the construction phase. Each fisherman was proud of his or her rod, because he or she had carefully chosen each piece so that it had an action that met his or her needs.

Unfortunately, all this inexplicably ceased one day. Telescopic rods replaced plug-in rods, and fiberglass took the place of wood. They are much more comfortable and less cumbersome when we carry them on our way to fish.

To be honest, I thought so too, plus they have nice colors and come in various lengths. But sometimes we don't realize that it is just a continuous catwalk in showing off our rods while we are fishing.

A wise proverb says, "The grass is always greener on the other side." Very often this is true; fishermen like other people's rods.

As the years go by, we all become collectors. Over the years we have always bought new rods, deluding ourselves that the next one would be the last.

New fibers have come on the market for rod construction such as Kevlar, which is three times stronger than steel and 20 percent lighter than carbon. Boron, which is stronger than steel and lighter than aluminum, and makes rods more sensitive and durable. And Carbon, which has exceptional lightness and total absence of vibration.

These fibers are ready to meet any need for the more advanced angler. The only sore point may be the price since they cost a lot and may not be affordable for everyone.

Sometimes, looking at and reflecting on all the series of rods that I too have bought in the past, a kind of form of repentance arises in me.

> *"Why did I buy all these rods? Why?"*.

With a lot of nostalgia, I still think back to my first wooden rod, made up of four plug-in pieces. It was the rod my parents gave me as a gift when I was 14 years old. Several times I have felt the desire to be able to have it in my hands again and fish with it once more to relive those old emotions of when it was really enough to have fun.

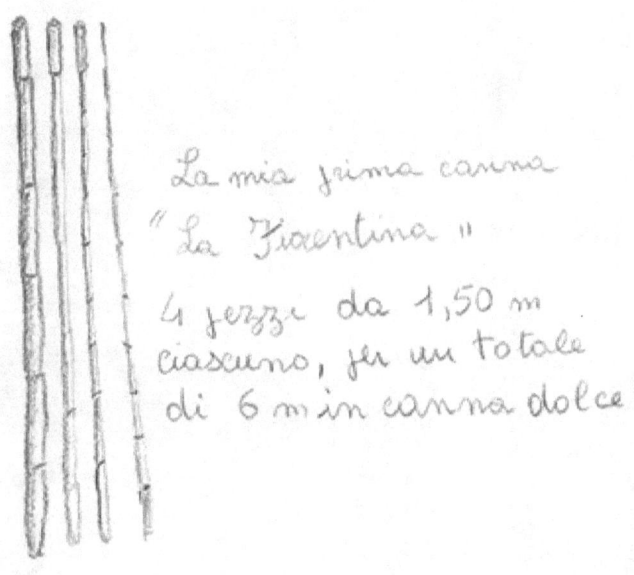

Fig. 3: *My first "La Fiorentina" rod. 4 pieces of 1.50 m each, for a total of 6 m in giant cane.*

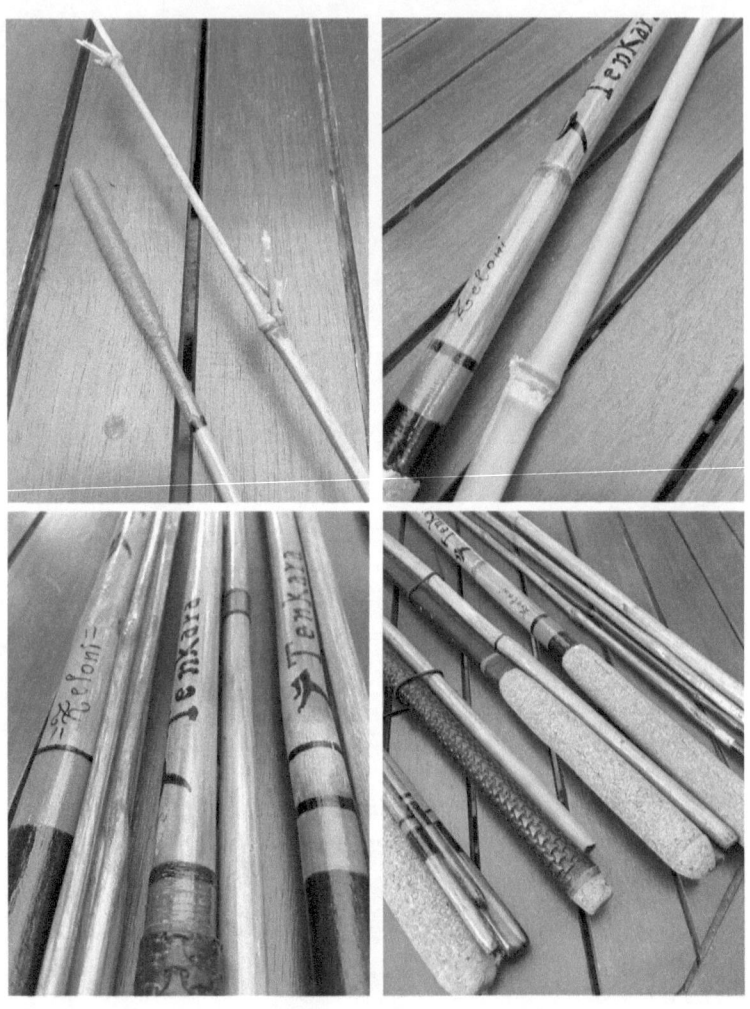

Fig. 4: *Some of my DIY bamboo rods.*

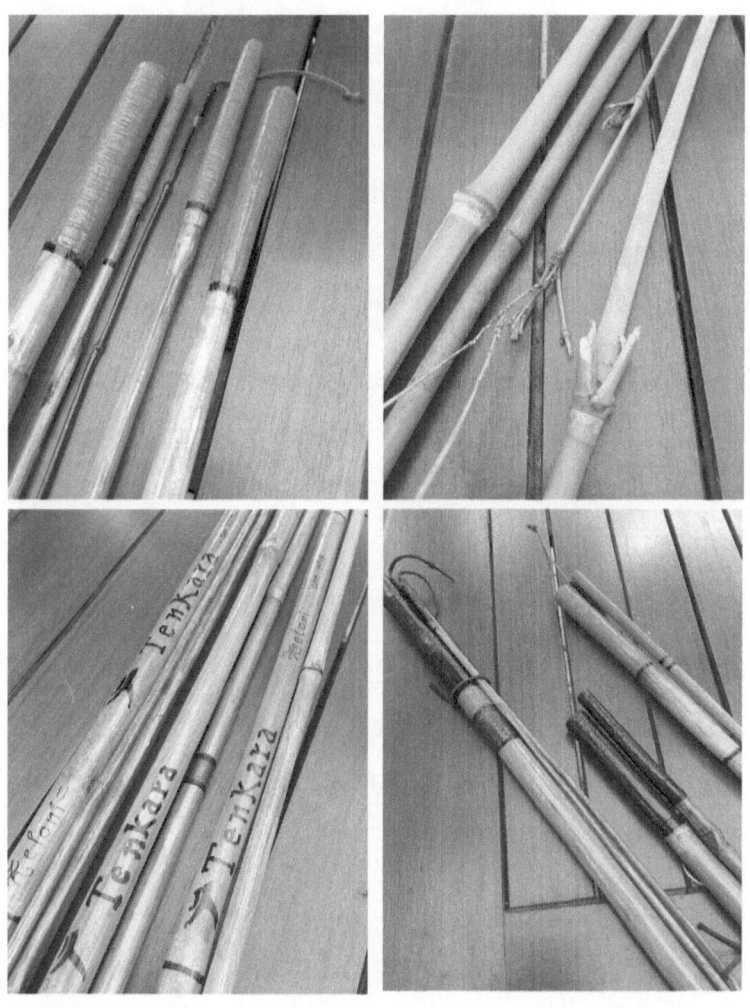

Fig. 5: Some of my DIY bamboo rods.

Modern Canes and Tips

We also find carbon-fiber tenkara rods on the market; they are telescopic and therefore are very convenient to carry. They have a footprint of only 54 centimeters and weigh less than 60 grams.

The lengths of these rods range from 320 centimeters to 400 centimeters. The 320-centimeter rods are fine for small mountain streams with little surrounding vegetation, while the 400-centimeter rods are fine for larger streams and rivers.

It must be calculated that the longer the rod, the more free space we must have around us when casting. We will thus avoid hooking the surrounding vegetation, including tree branches.

Each rod has its own action and it is expressed in the ratio of rigid to flexible parts. Example: if we find the words 7:3 on the rod, it means that the 7 lower parts of the rod are more rigid, while the other 3 upper parts are flexible. The most commonly used actions are 6:4 and 7:3. Of course, on the market we also find much stiffer rods with an 8:2 action or even very flexible rods with a 5:5 action.

This information on commercially available rods can be an inspiration for your own DIYs.

I will conclude with one more piece of advice. When we have finished fishing and are closing our rod, remember to be very careful with the thin parts of the rod, because they are very delicate. We will thus avoid possible breakages.

8.
Tenkara Lines

Casting a very light fly into the water is made possible by a simple string that can propel it forward by the weight of the fly.

This type of string is traditionally tapered, starting at a greater thickness and ending at a thinner one like the classic rat tail used for fly fishing with rods of English origin. Another widely used type of string is the level line, this one maintains the same thickness throughout its length.

We can find it commercially in convenient reels, and at the time of need we can easily cut it into the desired length, it is very practical and also cheap.

The level line, in the classic tenkara system, is as long as the length of our rod. To this on the final we will add a piece of nylon, also called tippet, ranging in length from about 1 meter, up to 1 meter and 50 centimeters, to which we will tie on the final our fly.

Personally, I have always used nylon finals of 0.12 or 0.14. The nylon end is to keep our stringer from being seen by the fish, and let's not forget that it should never rest on the water.

When we are dry fly fishing, we will have to keep the nylon up out of the water; only our fly will have to touch the water. Conversely, when we fish with a wet fly, we must let the nylon sink. Of course, in order to react promptly to the biting of the fish, we must always keep our fly hanging with the line under slight tension.

9.
The Tenkara Flies

We can say with full conviction that over the very long history of Tenkara, a great many artificial fly patterns have been used.

Each region of Japan had its own traditional patterns, somewhat like us in the West, where each region has its own traditions.

When we go fishing in a stream and we make good catches with a certain type of fly, what will we do the next times we return to fish in that place? Of course we will always use the same fly, because we have the confidence that it works since we have already caught fish there. So we will not have to worry too much in choosing the right fly, but rather we will have to pay close attention to how we present our fly in the water.

Laying it in the water must be very gentle, afterwards we have to bring it to life with very light calls, make it vibrate like a live insect that accidentally falls into the water and tries to get back up in the air.

A very versatile Japanese fly pattern is the famous Kebari – which would be more appropriate to call Sakasa Kebari – and the feature that differentiates them from others are the forward-turned hackles.

The Sakasa Kebari is thus a "reverse-hackle fly" with inverted hackles, and they are very simple to make. They can also be used in traditional fly fishing. We have already seen that it was originally created to be used in Japanese streams for fishing for native trout and char.

Another difference with our Western flies is that ours try to imitate real insects, while Sakasa Kebari flies are more attractive and impressionistic flies; they are pure fantasy flies that instead of possessing the shapes of a real insect, tend to have generalist traits allowing the fish to identify it as they see fit.

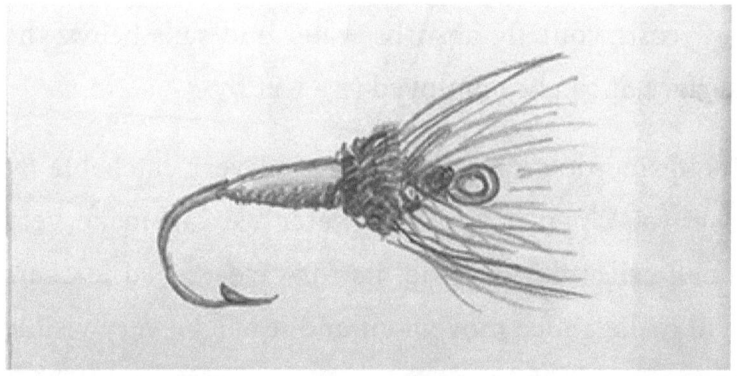

Fig. 6: *Kebari.*

As you can see from my drawing, the main feature of the kebari fly is that they have the hackles facing the opposite way from traditional artificial flies.

When we throw it into the water and recall it, the hackles pulsate giving the impression of a swimming insect. This movement is very enticing; it is irresistible to the fish. This fly does not imitate any specific insect, we can safely call it an ensemble or fancy imitation.

This pattern can be employed very well as a dry fly by gently resting it on the surface of the water. If after a few casts your fly absorbs water and sails below the surface, it can be employed as a wet fly.

Its upside-down feathers make it a very catchable fly pattern. When it is in the water we can make very small calls with our rod, its forward-turned feathers will make a nice movement and it will be very visible to the eyes of the fish.

Aquatic Insects

I want to tell you a little secret that has made my fly fishing work. It is very simple: I observed nature. Especially aquatic insects and the behavior of certain species of fish that feed on them. During a hatching - the metamorphosis of an insect from an aquatic to an aerial state – we notice a large flutter of insects around the water. Some insects swim for short stretches, others are swept along by the current before taking flight. Naturally, all this attracts fish that rise to the surface to gobble up these insects. Sometimes, with beautiful darts, the fish come out of the water to catch them on the fly, other times with the same frenzy they attack below the surface of the water. Observing all this spectacle will make it much easier for us to understand what kind of fly we should employ.

From our fly box we have to extract patterns very similar to the natural insects that the fish are eating. That is why observing nature is very important, it helps us to understand which insects we need to trigger on our rod. Of course they can be aquatic insects or terrestrial insects. We will look at the latter later on as well.

The aquatic insects we are interested in for tenkara fishing are found in these three major Orders found in every waterway: Ephemeroptera, Trichoptera, and Plecoptera.

Ephemeroptera

Ephemeroptera, also known as mayflies, include 2100 species of which about 200 are found in Europe.

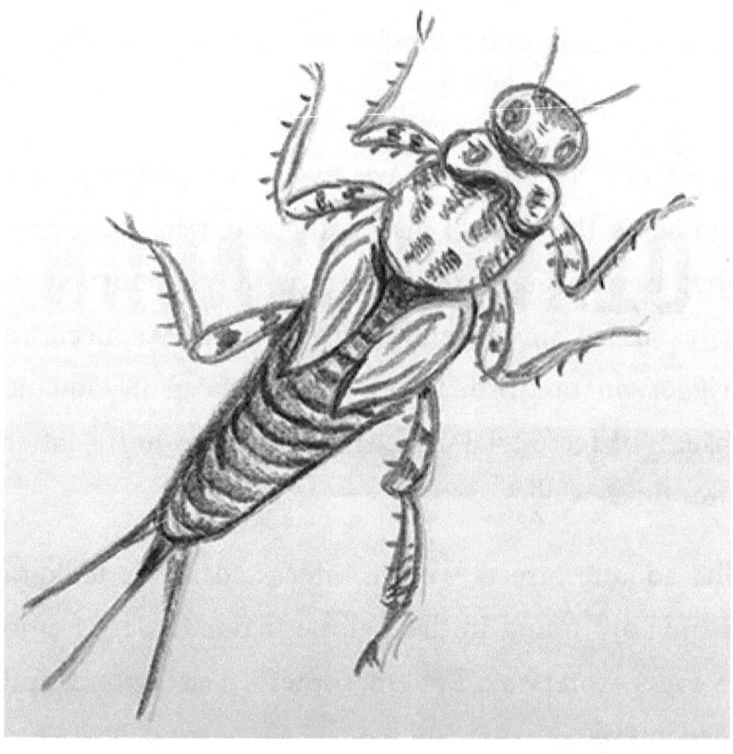

Fig. 7: Larva of ephemera that lives in water for a long time.

Fig. 8: *So it becomes the insect that has achieved metamorphosis out of water, its life will be very short. Some will live only for a few hours, others only for a few days.*

They have a very slender and delicate body, at the bottom of the abdomen we notice two or three caudal appendages. Their wings are often transparent and full of veins, and they possess four of them. The forewings are larger and more developed while the hindwings are smaller. When the insect is in the resting position, these wings are upright.

Trichoptera

Trichoptera number about 6000 species and are medium to small in size. They go from the initial larval state to the nymph state, after a certain period of time they reach the surface by swimming to perform the final metamorphosis.

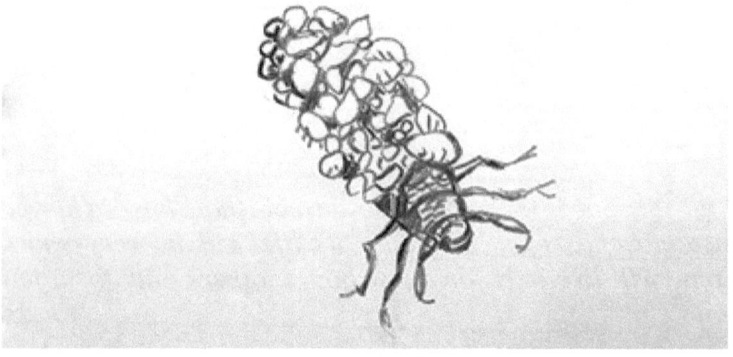

Fig. 9: Trichoptera larva.

The aerial life span of these Trichoptera is much longer than Ephemeroptera. In the adult state they have two very long antennae on their heads and possess four wings covered with very light down.

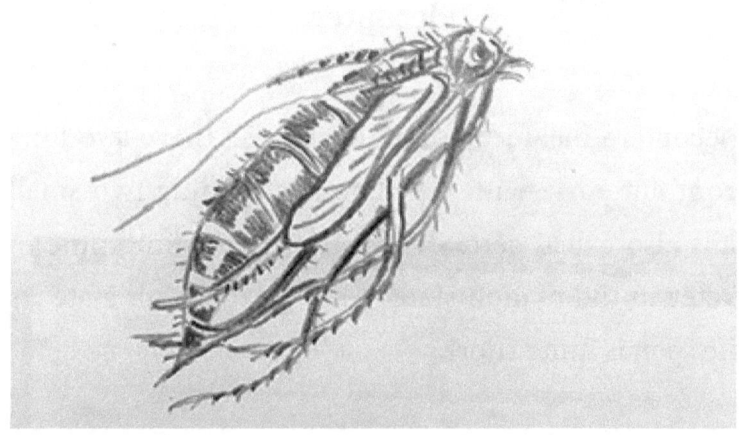

Fig. 10: Tricopter Nymph.

When the insect is in rest position it keeps the wings above the body in a sloping position with a characteristic "roof" shape.

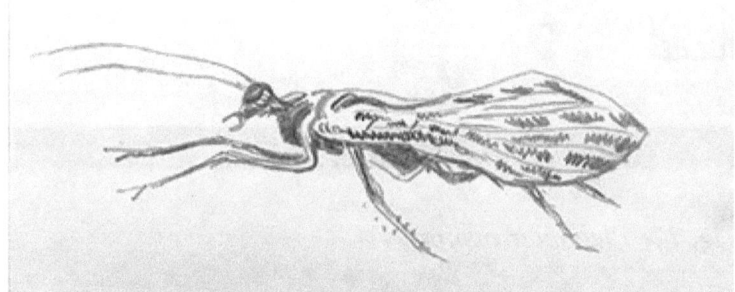

Fig. 11: Adult insect.

Plecoptera

Plecoptera include about 3000 species, have two long front antennae with the abdomen holding two small tails also called cerci. It lives for a very long time in water in the nymph state, while in the adult state its life span is quite short.

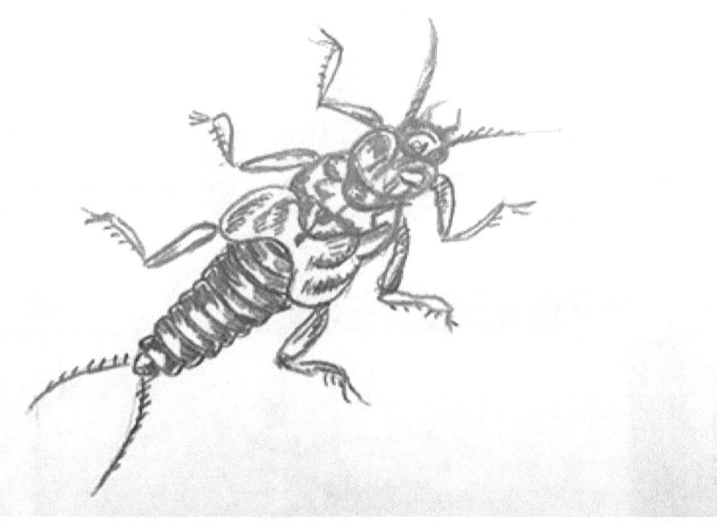

Fig. 12: Plecopter nymph.

The adult insect is small to medium in stature and has long, threadlike antennae. It has four membranous wings and in the resting phase they are horizontal and adjacent to the body.

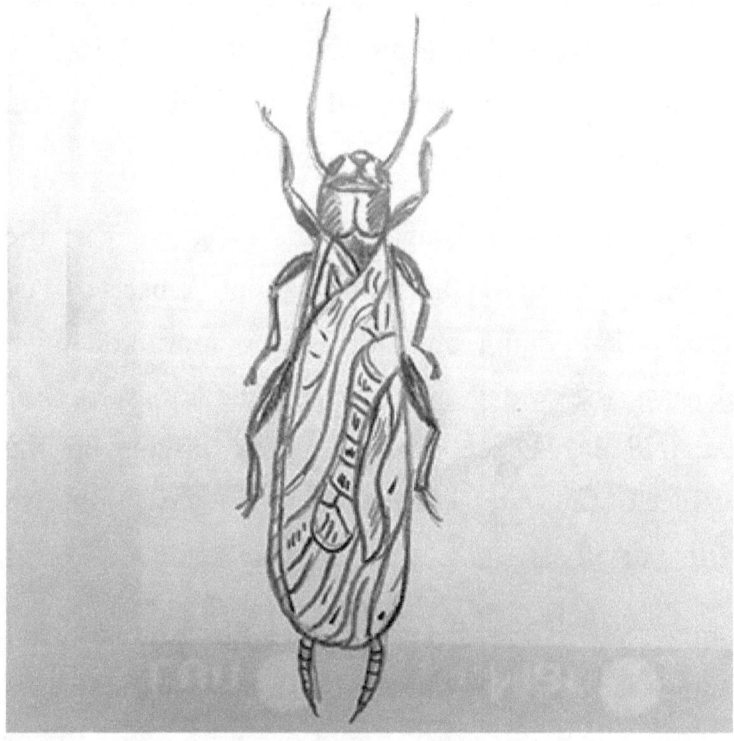

Fig. 13: *Adult insect.*

These insects after a long aquatic period as a larva or

nymph, rise to the surface and become adult insects, reach sexual maturity, and once they mate and lay eggs, the insect ends its life cycle and dies by falling into the water.

You must think about all these metamorphoses because these will indicate the most appropriate fly imitation, and the success of your fishing trip will depend on it.

These different life stages of the insect suggest the fishing technique you should adopt. Observe well what is happening on your fishing spot. You must observe the water and insect behavior well. For example, if we see insects causing circles on the surface of the water – so-called boils – we should fish with a dry fly.

Conversely, if the water will give the impression of being dead – that is, we see no fish boil and no insects fall into the water – we should fish with a wet fly, or nymph. In this condition, the fish are intent on searching the bottom for insects in their larval state to feed on them.

Now that we have taken a look at our dear aquatic insect friends, let's see how to use the various types of flies.

How to Use the Various Types of Flies

We have seen that in the tenkara technique kebari flies are used, the construction of which is very simple. But to help you refine your fishing even more, I want to introduce you to other types of flies that you can use.

They will come in very handy on your fishing trips. Of course, remember to observe the environment and pull out from your fly box the patterns that most closely resemble the insects that populate your fishing spot.

In addition to discovering them together, I will also give you some tips. For example, if we decide to fish with a dry fly and we notice that the waters of the stream in some sections are quite rough, it is advisable to use a fly with many hackles, even better if these cover the entire body. This type of fly is called a Palmer, it has good buoyancy and because of its flashy coloring with color contrasts, it will allow us good visibility as it travels in faster currents, thus enabling us to strike in the right time when the fish will attack.

We can mount them on hooks of number 10, 12 or 14. It is recommended to use white hackles for the hook head, for a total of 1/3, and for the other 2/3 use black and red hackles.

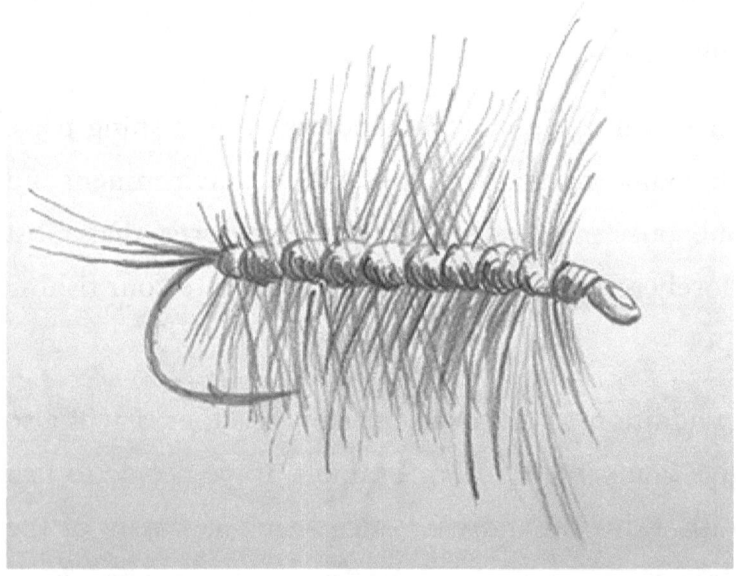

Fig. 14: *Palmer Fly.*

In calmer or even still waters, we can safely use our kebari, or a Tricoptera imitation if we have seen these insects flying. Tricoptera imitations are called Sedge; I recommend that you carry two types of Sedge with you: a light one and a dark one.

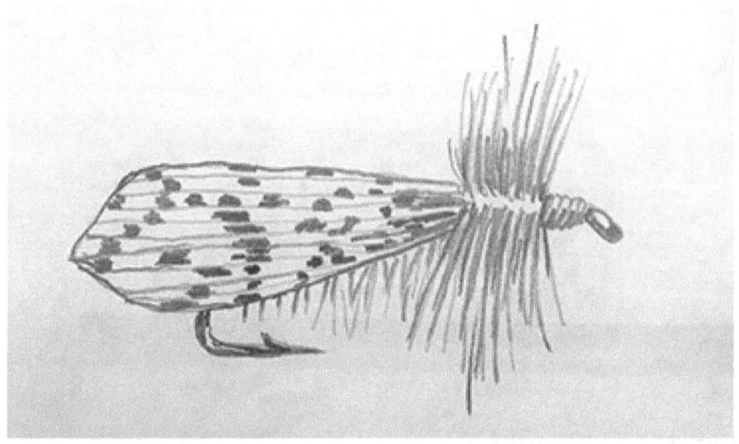

Fig. 15: *Sedge Fly.*

Of course, if you see ephemera, you can mount imitation ephemera. The most commonly used are these 5: Red Spinner, March Brown, Pheasant Tail, Blue Dun e Tups. These patterns will suffice for the entire fishing season. The shapes are almost similar to each other, what mainly changes is the color of the hackles and the thread used to construct the body.

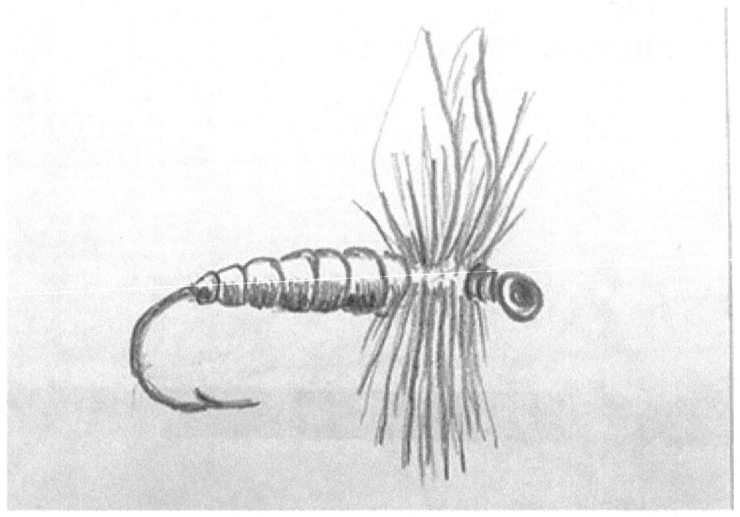

Fig. 16: *Ephemeral Fly.*

As time goes by, your experience will push you into building new fly patterns, let your imagination run wild, experiment with new colors and shapes. It is a lot of fun.

As we have also seen, the kebari is a very catchable

fancy fly, and any possible variation can do. However, always remember to pay attention to the color of the insect flies. We will have an advantage in catches if our kebari or homemade fly is the same color as the natural insect.

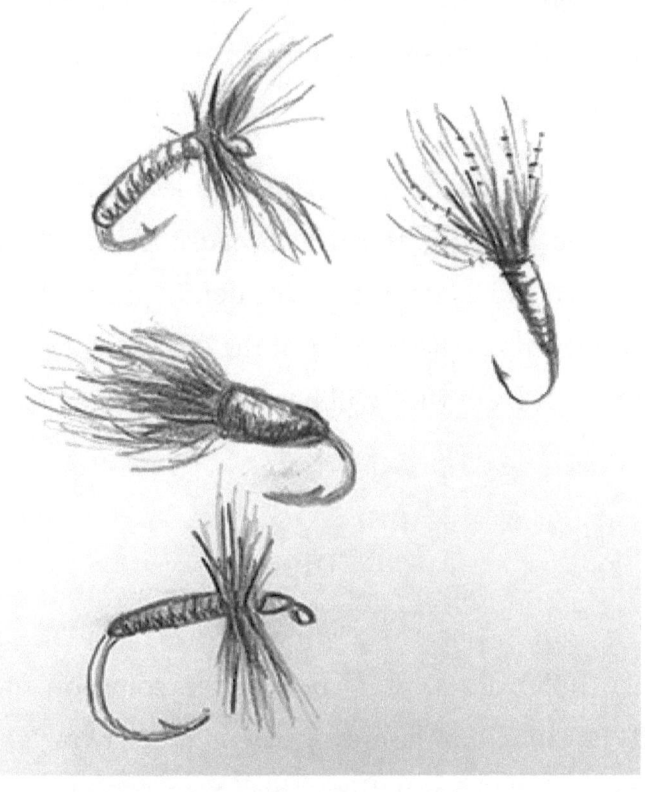

Fig. 17: *Kebari flies.*

Never stop training your spirit of observation. This will greatly increase your wealth of experience.

Terrestrial Insects

Terrestrial insects of interest to fly fishing are included in these two Orders: the Diptera and the Hymenoptera.

Of course, terrestrial insects are less important than aquatic ones for the fish, because their fall into the water is to be considered accidental. It may happen to find them on the surface of the water, where dragged by the current they will be attacked by the fish.

Diptera

To the Order Diptera belong the common flies that fly around our homes, gardens and lawns; they are the so-called house flies. These flies are equipped with two membranous and transparent wings, have large eyes, a rounded abdomen and are slightly hairy.

Fig. 18: Coch y Bondhu Fly.

Hymenoptera

In the Order Hymenoptera we find wasps and bees, their wings are membranous and the body is divided into three separate sections and they are: the head, thorax and abdomen. The legs are quite robust. Ants also belong to this order, but only winged ants are of interest for fishing.

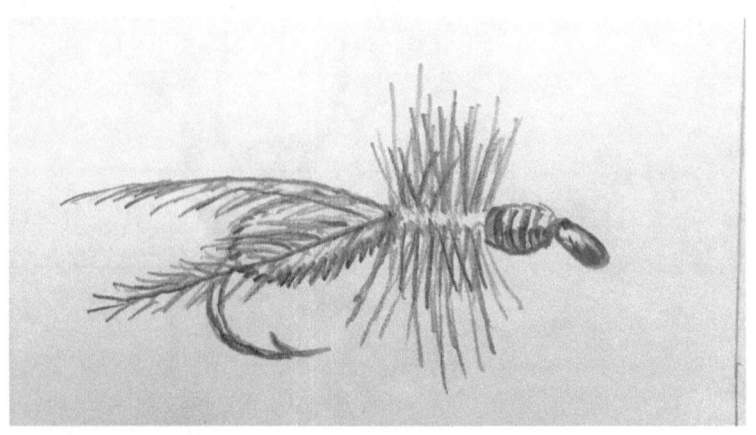

Fig. 19: Red Ant fly if red in color or Black Ant fly if black in color.

DIY Flies

DIY naturally involves saving money on fishing equipment, but that is not what makes it so special. DIY, especially during rainy or cold days that don't allow us to go fishing, makes us feel like we are fishing even if we simply stay in our corner, where we keep everything we need to build artificial flies.

We can imagine that what we are building will allow us to be able to make beautiful catches. Sometimes when I build flies I also imagine pleasant walks near mountain streams, while breathing in all the scents and various natural smells that only Mother Nature can give us.

Fishing after all, is also an opportunity to spend quality time in the heart of pristine landscapes where we lose the dimension of time. Is this not also the magic of fishing?

10.
Where to Practice Tenkara?

I told you about my personal experiences, we had a nice trip through the history of Tenkara and saw the flies we need to fish. I think many of you will now have a great desire to go fishing right away. Many of you must be wondering:

"Where can I fish in Tenkara? We are not in Japan, the nature and waters here are very different, even the fish are not the same. The technique is beautiful, but will it be possible to practice it in my area? In what way? In what waters?"

I will answer in a very simple way: the whole world is a country, all you have to do is want. Remember, want is power.

Not everyone in Italy can have the beautiful Dolomite streams at their disposal for a convenience, but don't worry, this is not a problem. With a little imagination we can easily fish in all those waters that are near our house, such as the small streams of our hills, the rivers and all those small lakes and streams on a plain.

Even if we don't find char, we can catch other very fun fish such as vaironi, chubs, and many other fish that we thought couldn't bite insects. You will be amazed at the discovery of all this. Fish safely where there is water, because where there is water there is fish!

Can you not believe it? Yet I assure you that this is indeed the case. Do not be influenced by those who say that a certain technique should only be practiced in a certain way, that it is only for certain types of fish or that it should only be practiced in certain waters, and that there are fixed rules that absolutely cannot be changed. These rules have only one function: that of limiting you.

Every angler must be free to be able to fish, freeing his or her fantasy both in equipment and in the way of approaching the waters, one must always dare and experiment and have his or her own personal vision of fishing.

Let me give you a small example, near my old home, there were small quarries and ponds, where I had never seen anyone fishing with artificial flies. In these ponds the most practiced technique was spinning, because the fish that lived there were mostly Black Bass. So many lures were used, the classic rotating spoon, undulating spoon, silicone lures and minnows were used.

I also used to fish with these lures, however, as I kept fishing in the same spots and always catching the same fish, I felt the need to change something to regain the enthusiasm of the first time.

So I started going to the same places over and over again, but I decided to change my fishing technique. Something told me to try fly fishing, and so I did. I still caught Black Bass, but this time with big homemade fly and dragonfly imitations. Fishing with a new technique in those spots, I rediscovered a new enthusiasm still experiencing new and fun emotions.

Now try to guess. In one of these ponds, after about a year, I decided to try a new and suggestive technique. I fished with a simple bamboo rod of just 4 meters. What was this technique? Tenkara, of course!

I caught the same fish, but I confess it was really a lot of fun and exciting. This confirms that all techniques can be good. In the same spot with different techniques I caught the same fish.

Think about it, after all the aim of a fisherman is to catch the fish, no matter what the technique used, but what really matters is playing smart with the fish while having fun. Even better if you respect nature and restore freedom to our finned friends of whatever species they are.

11.
How to Tackle the Creek the Right Way

Creek fishing, in my humble opinion retains in its entirety all the charm of Tenkara. It subconsciously resurfaces its Japanese origins, we immediately realize that we are fishing in a different way, a bit out of the time of our days. All this, I think, manages to convey to us without realizing it the true essence of fishing.

If we want to be successful in our creek, it will be helpful to know it very well. Before our fishing trips, let's scout ahead, walking curiously along the watercourse observing it carefully, scrutinizing its waters and all its natural obstacles, potholes and waterfalls with all its brisk runs.

It will be appropriate to scour every small hole, rock or small waterfall for fish, because even if we do not see them, it does not mean they are not there; they are just waiting to move at the appropriate time.

But always keep in mind one basic rule: that of learning not to be spotted by the fish!

Try to imagine where the prey may be. Here are some suggestions. Usually, fish will be found hiding behind stones or any other natural obstacle and will set up with their mouths facing upstream. This is because the current drags its nourishment downstream, and our fish will be there waiting for it.

Especially in the colder periods we will hardly see fish swimming in the faster currents, because at this time there are very few insects to eat, food is scarce, and only a few larvae dragged by the current might happen. The fish would expend too much energy swimming against the current, so in these conditions the fish will move very little. They will be in the calm and quiet nooks and crannies ready to move when any food source passes in front of their sight.

Walking in the creek is not always easy, sometimes the vegetation is very thick to such an extent that it prevents us from continuing, in which case we will have to go around it and look for an easier path. Sometimes it may happen that we are faced with a waterfall that denies us an ascent, again very calmly we will have to turn back and make a wide turn to manage to cross it.

It is important to know about these possible risks; we will need to be prepared when these mishaps might occur during our fishing trip. We will thus avoid wasting time unnecessarily.

The first thing to remember when we go upstream is that we must be very careful what we touch with our hands. We must never place them on a stone, or near a crevice without first observing it carefully. Just as we must never get into the bushes, if we haven't first moved them with the rod or with the boot, because there is a real possibility of being able to meet a bad customer: I'm talking about the viper!

Appropriate clothing will be useful for tackling the creek. I recommend wearing a good pair of amphibians or very high boots, solid velvet pants and a hat with a wide brim. A wide hat is useful because when we pass through vegetation it may happen that some insect, caterpillar or other small animal may fall on our heads and sting us or give us some irritation.

Get to know your creek well, study it thoroughly. Assiduous practice of a single watercourse leads after a few years to a total knowledge that will enable you to make good catches with greater conviction and ease.

You may find it useful to make a diary of your river, stream or any other spot. You can create mini journals where for each of your fishing spots you mark the flies that caught you the most fish. You can mark the time of year, note the colors of the flies and feathers you used. That way when you go back to those spots to fish, you will fish for sure.

12.

How to Tenkara Fish

Now that we have become familiar with our creek we can approach it in the right way and finally begin our desired fishing trip.

We know the route, we have seen whether our place is in the middle of vegetation or not, we know how much space there is from one bank to the other, and we have noticed some places where the fish are.

Well, now we can choose the size of our rod we think is appropriate, prepare our line and cast our bait into the water.

Our Tenkara Rod

Tenkara rods can come in a variety of designs, from ancient plug bamboo rods to very modern telescopic carbon rods. Some rods are three-piece, while others are made of several pieces but shorter, although the total length of the rod may be the same.

All of these models have a lanyard called a lilian at the top of the tip. A string called a level line is attached to the lilian. As we have already seen, both ancient Japanese and Valsesia fishermen used horsehair.

How to Prepare the Line

The length of the level line usually equals the length of the rod, rarely is a longer measurement used. At the end of the level line we will tie a piece of nylon as long as our open arms. Usually the thickness of the nylon ranges from 0.14 to 0.12. All we have to do at this point is to choose our kebari that we think is most appropriate, tie it to the nylon and start fishing.

As you have seen, it is very easy to rig the line. One of the many things I like about tenkara is that it allows us to tackle our creek with very minimal equipment, and this makes our journey much easier. In fact, as we have seen, we only need a simple bamboo rod, a string as long as our rod, a piece of nylon as long as our open arms, and a few flies.

This simple equipment is more than enough to be able to spend a nice afternoon in the proper spirit of Tenkara.

Casting

Now that our set-up is ready, we will approach the creek with plush steps, avoiding any kind of noise or sudden movement. If it is necessary to walk on all fours to hide from the sight of the fish we will do so. We must not get to the edge of the stream, but rather a few meters back. This is to avoid being seen by the fish.

At first we have to fish close to each other. So we will cast our fly at the beginning of the water. Then, cast after cast, we will move farther and farther until we get to the edge of the stream so that we can cast farther. In doing so we will sound out all the streams and fish refuges.

If after casting in one place for a while we find that the fish are not attacking, we can safely move somewhere else. We must not be in a hurry, but keep calm. We must carefully observe the new spot by imagining where we can find our finfish friend.

With our casts we will try to get our fly right in front of the fish's mouth, trying with a few lures to attract its attention so that we can induce it to make the attack.

Catch & Release

The sport fisherman always practices Catch & Release, which is to release the fish once caught. This to me is a noble gesture towards the fish, after it has entertained us giving it back its freedom is the least we can do. It would be best to use barbless hooks, they will allow us a faster and less painful release for the fish. Before catching the fish with our hand, it would be wise to wet it to avoid possible damage to the fish's skin.

I like to practice Catch & Release, it is nice to be able to watch the fish in our hand dipped in the water as we are releasing it. It is a wonderful feeling to see it go again, to follow it with our eyes until it disappears completely.

Unconsciously we are aware that we have established a deep bond between us and him, even if the fish will not be of our opinion, but we will always carry with us an eternal awareness of a contact that will never leave us.

Conclusion

Dear Fishing Friends, we have come to the end of our tenkara journey. I hope you have enjoyed it and that I have conveyed to you in the best way possible what I have learned during my fishing trips.

But before saying goodbye, I wanted to say a few words about our dear friend bamboo. We can fish with very modern, expensive, ultralight rods that will meet our needs perfectly, but the excitement and that old-fashioned charm that we thought no longer existed, we only find again when we fish with a simple bamboo rod.

It is amazing how immediately our concept of fishing changes. Suddenly everything changes. Time not only stops, but we are catapulted back in time. We feel transported to a different dimension, far removed from our usual consciousness. And suddenly, we are no longer in the little watercourse of our beloved hills, but have entered another dimension. Our little creek suddenly becomes special, it has become an enchanted corner of the world where we can take refuge, far away from an increasingly artificial society.

We experience a feeling of deep inner peace that suggests we should always continue to fish like this if we want to continue to savor the true essence of fishing.

Getting into full harmony with nature is the key. There are no secrets or taboos to be dispelled, only a logical path that unconsciously is showing us what is the right path to follow.

Thank you Tenkara! Thank you Dear Bamboo Friend! And Thank You Dear Fisherman Friend for reading these pages, too.

I hope to meet you on my next trip.

Lelio

SIMPLE FISHING WITH BREAD

The Secret?
Experience!

Lelio Zeloni

Bibliographical References

Boccardo, M. (n.d.). *Ami*. Essenza Pesca. Retrieved November 12, 2020, from https://www.essenzapesca.com/ami/

Boccardo, M. (n.d.). *Le Piume*. Essenza Pesca. Retrieved November 12, 2020, from https://www.essenzapesca.com/le-piume/

Boccardo, M. (n.d.). *Trenini e Mosche Valsesiane*. Essenza Pesca. Retrieved November 12, 2020, from https://www.essenzapesca.com/trenini-e-mosche-valsesiane/

Discover Tenkara, (n.d.). *Tenkara: la guida definitiva*. Retrieved June 14, 2020, from https://www.discovertenkara.com/tenkara-it/

Gaskell, P. (2020). *The Legendary Yuzo Sebata*. Tenkara Angler. Retrieved June 14, 2020, from https://tenkaraangler.com/2020/06/08/the-legendary-yuzo-sebata/

Lyle, M. (2019). *Tenkara Today*. Stackpole Books.

National Geographic, (2017). *La caza de osos de los matagi, una tradición sagrada y polémica en Japón.* Retrieved June 15, 2020, from https://www.nationalgeographic.es/historia/2017/11/la-caza-de-osos-de-los-matagi-una-tradicion-sagrada-y-polemica-en-japon

Pesca Network, (2011). *Pesca alla Valsesiana.* Pescanetwork.it Retrieved November 12, 2020, from http://www.pescanetwork.it/forum/index.php/topic/46196-pesca-alla-valsesiana/

Scalvini, A. (n,d,). *La canna per la mosca valsesiana.* Moscavalsesiana.it. November 13, 2020, from https://www.moscavalsesiana.it/it/blog/la-canna-per-la-mosca-valsesiana

Stewart, C. (n.d.). *Pesca Mosca Valsesiana.* Tenkara Bum. Retrieved November 12, 2020, from https://www.tenkarabum.com/pesca-mosca-valsesiana.html

Wigen, E. K. (1995). *The Making of a Japanese Periphery, 1750 - 1920.* University of California Press.

www.ingramcontent.com/pod-product-compliance
Lightning Source LLC
Chambersburg PA
CBHW030305100526
44590CB00012B/528